ALL THAT DIVIDES US

May Swenson
Poetry Award Series

ALL THAT DIVIDES US

poems
by

Elinor Benedict

UTAH STATE UNIVERSITY PRESS
Logan, Utah

Utah State University Press
Logan, Utah 84322-7800

Many of the poems published here have appeared in literary journals and other publications. A complete list of these is included in Acknowledgments.

Typography by Wolfpack.
Cover design by Barbara Yale-Read.
Cover art is a detail from a scroll painting by Song Feng Guang of Jinan, China.

Manufactured in the United States of America

Library of Congress Cataloging-in-Publication Data

Benedict, Elinor, 1931–
All that divides us : poems / by Elinor Benedict.
p. cm. — (May Swenson Poetry Award series)
ISBN 0-87421-295-2 (alk. paper) — ISBN 0-87421-406-8 (pbk. : alk. paper) — ISBN 0-87421-333-9 (e-book)
I. Title. II. Series.
PS3552.E53956 A79 2000
811'.54--dc21

00-009804

For the worldwide family
of
Grace Divine Liu

CONTENTS

FOUR: *Searching for Grace*

FOREWORD

When I undertook this brief introduction, I found myself in the refreshing position of not knowing the identity of the prize-winning poet, or where, or indeed whether, any of these poems had been previously published. Out of 728 manuscripts submitted, this one by Elinor Benedict surfaced as I read through the final completely anonymous twenty-five. On several subsequent rereadings, it rose again and again to the top.

Here are the facts about the poet that I learned afterward. Elinor Benedict lives in Rapid River, Michigan. Many of these poems have been previously published in journals ranging from *Helicon Nine* to the *Hawaii Pacific Review*, as well as in three chapbooks.

I was drawn to the narrative thrust of the book. The poet travels to China; she makes another and another trip. She and her daughter establish contact with missing relatives. These tentative rendezvous grow in intensity, and relationships develop from them. Although the poems stand as discrete units, they accumulate, taking strength from one another as we see them in their historical, chronological order. They grow on the reader as the narrative unspools, and we see the story told from successive points of view. It's an old story, full of poignant possibilities. "Don't you act so biggity, Miss Priss," Lula, the family maid, scolds. "Your aunt done married a Chinaman."

Nonetheless, an aura of romantic mystery shrouds this marriage from the poet's girlhood onward. The now aging aunt comes home to die, but the chapter never closes. Ultimately, the poet and her grown daughter travel to China to meet their Chinese cousins. Bits of the lovers' history, rescued from snapshots and old postcards, as well as face-to-face meetings with members of her family, spiral around.

Almost every poem delivers a sidelong irony, a study in contrasts that is always overridden by the sense of common humanity shared by two disparate cultures. In a poem titled "Ghost City," the poet is one of the tourists visiting Fengdu, a port city on the Yangtze River, where the dock is crowded with local entrepreneurs desperate to tell fortunes, or sell tangerines or finger puppets.

. . . a family
at the crowded dock presents their prize
boy with legs twisted backward, a blind
mother clamps her snot-streaked child
between her knees, all stretching out
their arms with trinkets. . . .

The poet's voice is clear, direct, yet artful. Many of the poems are written in nonce forms, stanzaic patterns that arise to suit the occasion. There's a skillful villanelle, but formalism is not the issue here. The sensibility that pervades these poems is that of a mature woman with an inquiring mind and a strong sense of family attachments.

Traveling from the airport with her half-Chinese cousin in his western suit, she begs him to explain where they are and what they are seeing. The bus inches its way down a street "choked with people waiting to buy cabbages."

. . . To just
such a market he used to rush, to wait
to buy pears for his mother. . . . beside me
my cousin makes a low sound in his chest.
Turning, I find his face drawn, white.
He whispers, "In the market I saw–myself."

The final poem in the collection, "For Those Who Dream of Cranes," in four sixteen-line, sonnet-like sequences, juxtaposes the white cranes of Jinan, China with the sandhill cranes migrating through Michigan, effortlessly playing one scenario against the other. In the final poem, the two tableaux come together:

Inside the maze, you learn the language,
begin the ceremony. Gray brothers,
fly safely. White spirits, speak.

Maxine Kumin

ALL THAT DIVIDES US

ONE

Begin the Ceremony

LETTER TO MYSELF ON MY BIRTHDAY

1 *June 4, 1931*

This is the day I was born.

Summer in Tennessee, a long time ago,
when people feared dust, debt,
and that dry mouth feeling the voice
over the radio's crackle called
fear itself.

In my mother's
hot room I lay naked and yelling
when my father's sister
came to say goodbye, holding
a baby of her own, half-Chinese,
leaving with a man
who changed her country,
her mind.

When I was older
I learned her story from snapshots,
gifts from abroad, bits of gossip
around the holiday table. I caught
those glances between my father
and my uncles, felt their
red-faced silence.

Lula the cook
served the meal as if she didn't
see. She took care of me, knew
the family secrets. How surprised
I was, to learn she had two
children of her own. When
my mother drove Lula home
downtown, two small boys
darker than their mother
ran up, then stared at me

through the closed
car window.

Once when
I wouldn't behave, Lula snapped,
Don't you act so biggity, Miss Priss.
Your aunt done married
a Chinaman.

2 *February 1974 - January 1980*

For years my world
seemed made of papier maché, yellowed
newspapers full of war stories
crumpled in a ball. I lost
my aunt's face among
armies and arguments, hid
her name in the fears I wanted
to forget.

Then one day a letter
rose from the mail thin as smoke,
strangely marked, a phoenix
among sparrows, announcing
she was alive, coming back
to die.

When she arrived, small
and gray, I was astonished
she could laugh. Her stories
of concubines and conquerors,
noodles and murders, brought
to my kitchen the underside
of the earth. Talk made us
sisters, remembering
younger days.

After her memorial
in the cold Hall of Martyrs,
her returned dust in China forever,
my cousins took me to see

the sights of Beijing, a careful
gift for American kin.

Quietly, proudly,
my cousins showed me the monument
where the death of Zhou Enlai
brought thousands of paper flowers,
black ink verses, to mourn
their loss of a father, more
than voices could say.

I stood
among strangers in Tiananmen Square,
winter all around, my aunt
in ashes.

3 June 4, 1989

Today I watch
Tiananmen Square from afar
flickering in a box, seething
in white June heat. Crowds gather
once more, sons and daughters of heroes
wearing faded jeans, headbands,
cocking their fingers
in the borrowed V. They push
a plaster goddess they hope
will save them.

Now they shout
those words we have heard so often
in our own language:
Freedom! Justice!

Lightning
nicks the air, smelling like
hot metal. The screen falters,
then flashes with the faces
of students marching. I want
to call out, *Wait! Take care.*
Breathe deeply. But they are born

in front of me, slim legs walking
toward the growling column
of tanks.

Then one small man
dares a tank to crush him. A cry
begins, the same cry we heard
in another stone place
filled with thousands of faces
of all colors, bearing
the eyes of brothers,
sisters–Listen!

The air
still vibrates with the voice
of that man whose dark face
shone in the downcast gaze
of Lincoln in his chair,
the voice of a servant
dreaming the end
of suffering–

Free at last!
Free at last! Thank God almighty,
we're free at last . . .

With the students of Beijing
I strain to hear him. His words
flow over us. Thunder rolls,
rain clatters, the earth
shakes as if it is opening.

Together, naked and yelling,
we are born.

A BRIDGE TO CHINA

In memory of Liu Fu Chi and
Grace Divine Liu

No engineer could dream
such arches, drape them over
monstrous pylons, ask armies
of ironworkers to hurl
enough highway across
a planet already curved,
tense with spilled rivers,
heavy with salt. Yet

one woman sailed across
more than an ocean
to join a man who dreamed
his country out of the dark.
Their lives spun silk
over distances, wove
legends of Sian's warriors
and tales of Tennessee
women, fine-tempered as steel.

Now their families face
each other across years
of long water, pull tight
between two continents
the invisible threads.

TO THE CHINESE PEOPLE, WHO SEE THE SAME STARS

Lake Michigan
lies flat in the dark
a black pool wide as a prairie.

The sky stands perpendicular
over the water's body.

Its tall onyx multiplies
the harbor lights
into a millennium of seeing

the clockless house of the hunter
the queen in her jeweled chair
the two bears eating
drinking, pouring

the everlasting cup.

TWO

Strangers and Kin

PAPER FLOWERS

Hall of Revolutionary Martyrs
Tianjin, China, January 14, 1980

An official hands out paper flowers. We pin them
on our coats, my daughter and I, following
our Chinese cousins into the Hall of Martyrs.
Cold flows from stone; an ocean closes behind us.
Our footsteps speak the only language we know:
Stop. Stop. We shouldn't have come.

*

In the anteroom we sip black tea. We try
to warm our hands on the cups while guests
fill the table like a jury. I bow my head, feeling
my daughter accuse me of mourning a woman I hardly knew.
Dear girl: She was my father's only sister.
You don't know yet, how that is.

*

The bald man beckons. We file into a chamber where
hundreds of gray flowers clutter the walls. From a hood
of black crepe her photograph gazes. I close my eyes.
Last time I saw her, the wind flew her hat like a kite
over the seashells, over the blue umbrella, at my father's
old house. She laughed when he caught it,
my father her brother again.

*

Four times we bow to her ashes boxed in a vault.
Men in gray suits collect all the flowers, stuff
them in cardboard for the next quick blooming. I'm dry
as the petals they crush, until someone touches my shoulder
like a small bird perching, an ivory woman in black. She takes
my daughter's hand, reaches for mine. She says nothing,
but her cheeks are wet, her eyes alive with the shock of love.

NEARLY

It's nearly twilight as our bus rattles
from the airport through narrow streets
on the outskirts of Beijing, dodging
shadowy pedestrians and scattering bicycles
like mice in a gray pantry. We rub

frost from the window panes with gloved
fingers and beg my half-Chinese cousin,
returning in his western suit, to tell us
what we see. He points out courtyards
smoky behind brick gates, small markets

choked with people waiting to buy cabbages
under yellow light. He says they hurry
to get home and dinner before dark. To just
such a market he used to rush, to wait,
to buy pears for his mother. We nod,

flutter our guidebooks and wave to children
in padded coats clustered like bells
beside doorways. Looking for familiar faces,
they keep their hands curved in their sleeves.
Workers stamp up and down in long queues

puffing the air blue with cigarets and cold.
At the curb a student ties green onions
to his bicycle, clutches a bag of pears.
He careens into traffic, trying to steady
an old woman against his back. Our bus

honks its way through the crowd. We press
our foreheads to the windows. But beside me
my cousin makes a low sound in his chest.
Turning, I find his face drawn, white.
He whispers, "In the market I saw–myself."

MEETING OUR CHINESE COUSINS

". . . every man heard them speak
in his own tongue."

–Acts 2:16

Pressed into a bedroom
of the Beijing Hotel
we are strangers

and kin.
We bow and hug
and give each other gifts

of sesame sweets
and tinfoil chocolate.
We take each other's pictures

and compare faces.
Everyone talks at once–
in two languages.

But I am confined
to a few words
like an expensive jailbird.

They feed me
the necessary phrases
bit by bit.

When they hand me
the key to my room
I go quietly.

But all night long
I sleep with my eyes open,
see hundreds of faces

listen for voices
speaking
in tongues.

TWO WOMEN LEAVING BEIJING

We follow the evening tide that pulls
us through the railway station's
halls like seawater sucked
into caves. Dazed by the swell,
I see myself among swarms
of fish–one small neon among
swirls of dark silver. They flow

around me like chains, hauling
their burdens from earth's center
where almost everything sleeps.
We inch toward a stairwell, ooze
through its narrows, fan out wide
to a bay where black trains
fume and sigh. At last we grow

legs, walk upright, breathe.
I notice a woman hurrying beside me
the shape of my mother, dangling
a carp in mesh, its body frozen
in weather. I start to live

in her clothes. My son,
his wife and two little ones
shiver in our upstairs room,
anxious to see me thaw out
the prize, stir a white batter,
heat up the stove–but I can't

finish this scene without seeing
my own son, tall, his jaw bearded,
his blue eyes keen, grinning
beside his car with a salmon
hooked on his thumb. Just then

the woman stops, swings her fish
up the steps of the train as I pass
on to mine. She hesitates as if
I had called her and turns
at the door. We look

toward each other like migrant
women of two different tribes,
tending separate fires, clutching
our skins around us, rising to see
who comes.

IMMOLATION OF A STRANGER

for Ellen Liu (1937–1983)

It's jade, flawed with brown flecks,
rimmed with narrow gold and not quite
the shape of our usual hearts, those
valentines with twin scallops we send
to hide and seek love. This one,
cool as a lilac leaf but heavy
in my hand, grows a third curve
where the chain holds—an odd
catch of the heart.
                                        I close my fingers
around the green stone, remembering
the chilly gift shop in Beijing
where bored young women sold
silks and bamboo off-season. They
hugged themselves in the bitter air
and turned their heater's flame so high
I imagined the fringe of my plaid
wool scarf catching fire for buying
something cheap to take home.

Ellen, my cousin and companion
that final day, watched me solemnly
as I made my small choice, guided me
with kindness through that gray city
she called home, looking even then
as though she were lost. Her eyes
and forehead—half foreign, half family—
made my face burn as I remembered
how my uncles, their necks flushed,
talked about their sister marrying
a Chinaman, disappearing for years,
only to come back at the end
to make claims on them.

But gentle Ellen,
who owned so little, claimed nothing
but what I felt from wearing
her mother's face.
Now three years
later this thin letter from Beijing
tells me how the same grim illness
and death that took her mother,
my second self, has finished her.
I think of journeys, kin, distances,
home. Foolishly I wonder what
she took with her. If I could
send her something, I'd say, Ellen,
take this, my flawed stone heart,
and keep it green.

HAWTHORNS

At the Temple of Heaven
old men with tightened faces
sell sticks of small red haw-apples, pierced
by the dozen and glazed over fires. I buy them

like beads with my newly-changed money, fumbling
in cold, counting out coins and mixing
white breath with incense
of charcoal. My Chinese

cousins watch as I bite
the sweet skins, the tart fruit, full of seeds
hard as mahogany, clinging to each other
in carved families. Nini, the eldest,

looks into my face as we climb
the temple's great stair and says in her soft
syllables: Those were the favorite
fruits of your aunt, our mother,

when she was still
with us. Do they grow in America
where you live, where once she lived as a girl?
Here, the same hawthorns bloom white in spring,

and when their petals fade, the harsh yellow
wind from the desert blows them
over our rooftops like fine ashes that fly

almost as far as the sea.

CITY OF DUST AND WATER

Tianjin, China, 1980
Damaged by earthquake, 1976

1

The dry earth coughed, shrugged, dropped
its load of buildings into cracks
that opened with sounds of stone
grinding on stone.
                    Underground
kingdoms rumbled their doors, scrawled
their messages on walls. Neighborhoods
broke into anthills, running with fathers
searching for families, everyone
turning to children in earth's
quick coming apart . . .
                    How slowly
the signs of a city's undoing erase.
The people of Tianjin do not boast,
"Here is the tower that fell,
the ancient cedar uprooted."
They look down, brush away
dust. It settles everywhere,
in hair, in eyes. Their voices
squeeze out of lungs still
choked with surprise.

2

Sampans toss and groan under our hotel window.
At 2 a.m., my daughter and I cannot sleep
together in this bed so many worlds
from home: our snow-hushed rooms, warm
and separate, changed to this stiff
intimacy under silk. Neither of us knows
the other's skin. Hers is smooth, blue as milk;
mine crinkled, scalded cream. We try
not to cough or sway the ancient mattress.
But I want to tell her how this dark

hotel's a buried city of women like us.
In this room we meet and part from our
mothers, children, lovers, breath.
This bed swings like a bridge
over all that divides us.

THE GUEST CHAIR AT NANKAI UNIVERSITY

First we dine on carp, sweet and sour.
After the prized fish, the old chairman
slurps his soup. Hunched like a holy man,
he never looks up from his bowl. But the Canadian
exchange professor stares at me between
spoonfuls and rubs his new beard. Over

green cabbage and leeks he tells me
his students of English beg him
for lectures on Adam and Eve,
Jesus and the fishes. He says these stories
filled his childhood in Saskatchewan
by the parsonage stove. Now they
haunt his cold narrow room. And what

does he tell them? Parables
in whatever words he can find. Then
the students ask if his people really
believe. They write out dozens of questions
on Bible-thin paper. Across the teacups
choked with leaves, the professor hands me
pages like white money, trembling.

During the passing of pears I study
the students' small writing. Who is God?
Why did he make the world? What does it mean
to be saved? I think these are the same
questions asked by strangers who sweat
in cold rooms. Before I can

find out what answers
he gave them, it's time to rise
from a table littered with fish bones
and bow to a chairman sleepy with meat.
I shake the professor's hand and say

the only thing I can think of
to join us together: *Good luck
fishing!* His eyes look
hungry for more.

CHINAVISION

1

Still I see those two-humped camels
tied for tourists at the sunny hut
beyond the shadow of the Great Wall.
Blond girls stare and run toward
the arch, hugging their blue nylon
ski-jackets. Cold burns their cheeks
with crimson stars. I follow them,
sand in my eyes, as wind swoops
like a comet's fist, socking
my breath away. Above, the wall
crouches on yellow mountains, teeth
crumbling, no longer sharp against
barbarians. On the parapets old men
in Mongolian hats grin and offer
chunks of jade hidden in rags. Blinded,
I shake my head, fight to the last
tower, wondering why their ancestors
wanted this wind, this wilderness;
how thousands of hands could fit
these stones with freezing thumbs.

2

Later, afternoon sun tries to warm
the Valley of Mings, where 13 emperors
buried themselves under 13 hills.
Two camels, chiseled in stone, face
each other on the Avenue of Beasts,
smiling for their photographs. My half-
Chinese cousin stands beneath two smooth
humps and squints in the sun, ready,
but my camera jams in the cold. I must
carry this picture in my eyelids, back
to another continent, this house
where I reel in gray visions. I see

my cousin beside the strange beast,
his twin, wincing in the glare;
and afterward, his face reflected
in the train window as he returns
to his old city, his skin pale,
his lids closed. Now both of us
see double under a single sun,
our eyes full and burning.

STORYTELLER

for William Weihan Liu

It's your story, cousin, but I've
stolen it. Like a magpie I've snatched
pieces of your life to weave a coat
for myself, more colorful than a wise
father would have given, something
I made and called my own. They're

all gone now. Your mother, your
two sisters, your own engineer father
who used to take you with him Sundays
when you were a boy to check the city's
vast water system, his greatest pride,
next to his only son. You still

keep the small yellowed snapshot
of the two of you pausing in ritual
inspection tour, your father's face
broad and competent, yours small, thin,
but both smiling, pleased in each other's
company, safe after a world at war

in your own city. Your birthright is your
vision of all that happened since, China
in extremis through your eyes as a boy
with feet straddling both worlds,
a story you will write for yourself
someday, when time tells, spirits rest.

For me you are generous with your life.
You will not give me away. Only I
can do that, a loving thief giving
fingered goods back with a pinch
of rue. Here in my patched coat,
my pretender's shoes, I stand.

THREE

In the Company of Magpies

THE CHINESE ART & CULTURE TOUR

Valuables

In Shanghai rich young Amanda buys dead insects
in amber from a shop as dark as a vault.
Where jade cutters hunch, she scoops up
handfuls of stones, raking them into her purse,
twittering how they look just like quail's eggs.

At the carpet factory she picks out a rug
swarming with dragons, nestled in wool too white
for anyone else to afford. She rolls it up
like a sausage, so many dollars per pound.

Later, in a town full of farmers, she yawns
through schoolrooms, fidgets through institutes,
hurries to prowl the back streets for more loot.
Soon she comes running, her eyes big as bowls.
"It's true! They do eat rats. An old woman
grinned and offered me one by the tail!"

"Tut," says the guide, descendant of Wu, king
of this province famous for gardens and silk
and small-fingered girls who embroider cats.
He smiles with centuries of charm: "The people
of Suzhou want foreign ladies to know
how well we take care of pests."

Mischief

In the Forbidden City
under a cold dazzling sun
we take pictures of men
in fur hats grinning,
showing jagged teeth
and breathing out frost
like smoke from campfires
hidden under rough coats.

Kin to the Khans, these
men with tawny faces come
from provinces up north,
teased by forbiddance,
tickled to be tourists
in their wildest outfits
for curious western
women with cameras who
giggle, find them irresistible,
and go *Click! Click!*

The Look

In the upstairs jade factory
young men and women in gray suits
bend over drills and emery wheels
to shape gardens of green stone.
They look like machines themselves,
faces blank, fingers moving as if
oiled and geared. They stop only
to exercise their eyes to a recorded
march with scratchy, barked commands.
Then quickly they resume chiseling
ornate leaves, birds, phoenixes
that look as though artful monks
on a mountaintop carved them
with years of meditation.

They were picked, we learn,
for their dexterity, spatial knack,
ability to follow a plan. Their workplace
is cold as a cave. In back of the room
near a stove that gives barely enough
heat for fingers to move, one young man
suddenly looks up. While the others
keep on carving, his eyes lock
onto mine. Insolent, hot. He wants
to throw down his flowery statue,
stalk toward me and grab my wrist,

push me down into his chair behind
mountains of frozen stone, hissing,
"Work, you lazy white dog!"

Bamboo

Off a back street courtyard, a gray room
flowers with bright brush paintings
by elderly men and women who gather
to meet us. They wear old Mao suits
as if they have slept in them for years.
They sit shyly while their leader demonstrates
how to paint bamboo on silk.
                                        But we are tired.
We have seen too much bamboo already.
During the question period we hardly ask
anything. We walk around slowly, smiling
at the walls, wondering what these people did
before they got old. Worked in the silk mills,
picked soybeans? One small woman shuffles
up to me and points out her painting above us,
a blood-red peony. She tells me she speaks
a little English. I look for a suitable
question to give her.
                                "What did you do
before you retired?" She bows her head as if
receiving a blessing, answers, "For China
throughout seven provinces I designed
railroad stations. Also my design,
this next picture of bamboo."

The Wild Dinner

Chinese city dwellers call far-out Guilin
wilderness. Ancient poets and painters
grew blissful over its sugarloaf peaks,
clouded shrines, criss-cross thickets
of pine and bamboo that fueled the mists
of their minds. Later, half a century ago,

these limestone caves proved useful
in hiding from bombs. Refugees huddled
where we now stand. Today the travel bureau
jazzes the caverns with red and blue lights,
applies nicknames that out-do Disney
for tourists, the newest frontier.

Tonight's farewell feast is billed
"The Wild Dinner." In a private room
above untamed peasants we drink strange
beer, sing loudly what sounds like
Sino-American hillbilly. When
twisted meats of mysterious origin

arrive steaming, our guide translates
with difficulty. This is–how you say–
the delicious "flying fox." We munch,
guessing squirrel. Other beasts we leave
tangled in rice as we swallow fiery
maotai, toasting South China wildness.

Months later the flying fox leaps out
on Sunday afternoon TV, flexing its black
wings, grinning like a miniature hyena:
the notorious giant fruit bat of Southeast
Asia. As its leathery body flops before me,
I redefine my ability to adjust

to wild things.

Partings

We applaud over littered banquet plates
and Qingdao beers, start loudly singing
American camp songs mixed with Chinese ditties
hardly anyone understands, but everyone
keeps grinning and toasting Mr. Yi.

Mr. Yi is leaving home to be married.
He is bashful. After more songs, his face
grows damp as Mr. Yang, his fellow guide,

presents him with a wedding gift:
a bed comfort of bright red silk.

Asked to solo, Mr. Yi demurs, hangs
his head, mumbles when his friend
calls his voice the best in the province.
But later, on the way back to the hotel,
as the darkened bus rocks us to sleep,

a quavering tenor rises against silence.
This is no brazen shriek of Chinese opera.
It's a child lost. An animal snared. We
clutch our sweaters around us. After the wail
subsides, Mr. Yi tells us under dark's cover

the name of his song from ancient China,
"Saying Goodbye to a Friend." In our light
applause I seem to hear the sound of water
lapping against the sides of our bus, a boat
full of strangers, pulling away from shore.

SYLVIA PLATH IN CHINA

How did you get here, big blonde
with x-ray eyes? On the train
from Jinan to Qufu, you climb out
of a slick magazine brought by an old
classmate of yours from the States
who wants a place in the gossip.

Today you wear a new mask, cold
and arrogant, no longer pitied for
your faithless husband, your lone frenzy,
two little children left to find
bread and milk instead of mother.
If you had lived, maybe you'd ride

this train as a gray-haired grandma
with children in your billfold,
scribbling your latest volume since
the Pulitzer, with a kindly second
husband dozing at your arm. Green
fields of rice blur by. You smile

at hyperbole in a teacup. The house
you'll return to is warm, ordinary,
with all the conveniences you missed.
If your immortality didn't depend
on misfortune, mania, and death
at an early age, squeezing genius

out of your brain like grapes
pressed to thorns and sour wine,
we could welcome you home.

GHOST CITY

That's what they call Fengdu,
mountainside river port in midday mist
where tourists stream from the white ship
up a long stairway from the Yangtze
slippery with ages of black mud. We watch
our feet carefully, look down as hands

reach out with tangerines, postcards,
green rocks, toy cars. We know how
to steel ourselves to women's cries
shrill with the word they believe
is magic for tourists, *Hello! Hello!*
shouted like caged parrots who

expect no answer. We turn away,
boarding the bus for a mountaintop
theme park based on Sichuan folklore,
where a lipsticked guide singsongs
American slang as she leads us
through ancient pagodas of 1985,

guarded by concrete monsters crude
as a kid's gory scribble. We push away
peddlers with bloody finger-puppets,
refuse to heed forecasts of happiness
depending on how we cross a bridge,
balance on a wooden ball. Where's

our sense of humor? Gone. And when
we come down to the river again, a family
at the crowded dock presents their prize
boy with legs twisted backward, a blind
mother clamps her snot-streaked child
between her knees, all stretching out

their arms with trinkets. *Hello!* Why
do the people of Fengdu seem more
desperate than those of a dozen other

Chinese cities we have seen? Is it because
their crumbling homes will be covered when
the great new dam starts holding back

the river? Or is it just their fear of
any tomorrow? As we slowly disappear
into the white boat, we are mute, looking
back at the clustered shore, remembering

what little we know of Hell, thinking
that in this place we are the ones who are
unreal. We are the ghosts of Ghost City.

THE TRUTH ABOUT HISTORY

Where Were You?

At Shandong University a middle-aged
professor wearing a pinstriped suit gives
his lecture on "Modern Chinese History
for Foreign Visitors." The room feels
muffled as he details the May 4 Movement,
Mao's rise, the Japanese War, Liberation.
We nearly fall asleep, but we wake up when
he reaches the Gang of Four, nearing that day
we saw on television, Tiananmen Square.

He stops before he gets there. We ask him
why. He clears his throat, pronounces
the incident too new to be history. Then
he offers what he insists is only his personal
opinion: Lawless elements, vandals to blame.
We glance at each other. Afterward someone asks
our young Chinese guide if he agrees. His eyes
cloud. He begins as usual, "A very difficult
question." He looks behind him and quick
as a tossed grenade, blurts, "I was there."

Cleaning the Stain

Chinese toddlers wear open-air pants,
a scandal to westerners, but practical.
A young mother in mini-dress, chrome yellow
with black polka dots, shiny high heels,
turns her back on her squatting son,
who pees baby-style on pavestones.
An old woman passing by clucks approval
at the boy, not at his mother, who
walks away, pretends he's not hers.
Soon the boy scampers back to her side,
begs a bottle of Sprite, then runs

to pour it on the widening spot. She turns
her back again, putting on dark glasses.
It's simple enough to clean that stain,
one of many. Others are not so easy.

HOW TO CHANGE A COUNTRY

At the Peasant Movement
Institute, Guangzhou

The Belt

How spare this place is:
A monastery turned into cells
for Mao's early converts,
learning how to change
the country overnight,
over months, over years,
however long it took.

Everything is in rows:
Narrow beds, earthen bowls,
tables of rough wood.
Nothing is wasted,
nothing says comfort.

And in Mao's own cell
there is something else:
a holster and cartridge belt,
looking ready, hanging
on a peg like a coat
waiting for him
to come back.

Outside the institute
Mao's statue, not yet
toppled, stands huge
among cherry trees:
a stone man–too big
for his belt.

The Memento

On the institute wall
we find a small photo
in black and white
of those who studied

here, among them
handsome Zhou Enlai,
a shadow-man who often
stood between Mao
and the people.

I ask my Chinese cousin:
Why no giant statue,
no florid portrait
of Zhou? At first
he doesn't answer.
Then he says only,
It's not his way.

Meaning, I think,
Cousin, be quiet.
You walk on our soil,
but you cannot enter
that needle hole
inside us where
he lives.

YIN AND YANG

Shanghai Contortionist

She's at it again, that rubber girl
with no bones. Look how she bends
slow as a snake, sitting on her own
head and grinning between her legs

at the crowd who loves it. In the wings
her master waits. The laundry needs doing,
rooms want cleaning, a dozen guests
are coming for Peking duck. She

balances five tiers of crystal
goblets on her chin while she rotates
like the world on its axis, knows
he will want her later, using

her most exotic positions, torso
and legs presented like fine loins
of beef to be turned, twisted,
pounded into succulent display.

Young Tai-Ji Master at Qufu

Is it the white silk of his loose
shirt and pantaloons sliding against
his still-cool brown body

Or is it the tight skin of his muscled
neck, small-knotted at the throat
between tendons like cords

balancing the chiseled head and face,
eyes cave-black, watching a distant
fire that never burns out?

Or is it the movement itself, slow
as a hidden river flowing soft over hard
stone to the ocean's floor like a net

that dredges us out of ourselves,
makes us part of this man turned oracle,
mind and body prophesying together?

MR. YUAN'S TWO JOYS

Our Chinese guide adores English idioms.
He presents them to us like bonbons
at each corner we pass in Shanghai,
where old men play chess at rickety
tables between their knees. When
the bus stalls in thick traffic,
Mr. Yuan scratches his head, declares,
Gridlock! and smiles for the first time.

At the park Mr. Yuan makes a speech
about Liberation, how before that day
signs said, *No Chinese and Dogs Allowed.*
He puts his palms together, offers:
Birds of a feather flock together?
This time he doesn't smile. We clear
our throats, look out the window.

Next he takes us to the section
where he says beggars, opium addicts,
prostitutes once crammed the streets
like dead fish. *Redlight district,*
he intones, waving to an empty plaza,
now clean as whistle with communism.
We wonder whether to smile or frown.

While we visit the museum, Mr. Yuan
stays outside by the bus, chain-smoking.
Like a smokestack, we could say
as we return, looking him over secretly
at close range. He is small, young-old;
his chiseled face looks *dog-tired.*
A former professor, maybe, or a diplomat.

When the tour is over, we ask Mr. Yuan
how he will spend the rest of his Sunday,
expecting him to tell about home, family.
In the park, he answers instead, *playing chess.*

He smiles his second smile, almost radiant.
Quietly we file off the bus, leaving him
in the doorway. We whisper to each
other: *Do you think they tortured him?*

CHINESE PUZZLE

You say they've been civilized
longer than anyone, and this museum
proves it, with artifacts made
thousands of years before Christ:
implements, weapons, remnants
of that famous potentate in Sian
who loved his warriors into clay . . .

Consider the intricate casting
of this bronze dagger, the iris blue
porcelain, red cloisonné peonies
growing on the mirror of a palace
concubine. What is the link
between art and cruelty? Here
are the makings of war, slavery,
and notions of beauty that crushed

girls' feet into pairs of dead lilies.
See how exquisite the small shoes.
Like you, I could rave about loveliness
but instead I ask myself where
goodness and justice fit in. You'd
touch a finger to my mouth and chide,
Don't ask. Let civilization
make beauty without judgment . . .

Take this scroll, for example,
with cragged mountains, lone monk
by a cave. Observe the wet pines,
raven in mist, waterfalls lighting
the monk's smile. A courtier
imagined this wilderness among
tassels and brocade. Did either
painter or painted hear the muffled
weeping in the narrow passageways
that twisted into the city's heart?

FULL MOON HARVEST FESTIVAL AT THE SPA CITY

In the restaurant and all over China tonight
there are millions of mooncakes, flat and round,
white with mysterious dark centers.

Here in this luxury retreat built for him,
aging moon-faced Mao never quite arrived,
never climbed the three hills or dipped

in the seventy-two springs that dried up,
or swam in the Olympic pool still waiting
without ripples behind glass walls.

Now among second-level bureaucrats driving
Japanese cars, our study group steps
from a minibus, inhales the bourgeois roses.

Beyond the hotel's blue-lit fountains,
exotic pines and pagodas loom at dusk.
Then an enormous moon appears.

Next morning at the prison seminar
we taste mooncakes fresh from the oven.
The warden breaks them apart for us

at the kitchen door after his lecture
on all the lies our press tells about
Chinese prison labor. Fuming,

the torn cakes reveal their dark secret
and we agree, they're the best ones
we've eaten. We lick our fingers

and proceed to the last courtyard,
where a small brass band of prisoners
breaks into "Auld Lang Syne." We wave

goodbye with mooncakes on our breath,
believing most of what we have heard
in hope of a fortunate harvest.

PEACE ROAD KINDERGARTEN

In this small city within a city
children live from early morning
until dusk, when parents come back
to remind them who they are. All day
they chatter like flocks of sparrows
who used to nest, the oldest teacher
remembers, in these low trees with shiny
leaves, before all birds were eaten.

Today for foreign guests the children
dance and sing under red tile roofs
where the air smells like jasmine
and cabbage soup. They dress up
in festival costumes with paper flowers,
silk butterflies, golden crowns,
crane feathers. For the grand finale
two boys roar in a double dragon suit.

Sweaty after the pageant, the children
troop outside, strip to underpants
and swim two by two in a raised pool
the size of a victory garden. Some
children's ribs show, none looks fat enough
for a dragon to eat. But they are strong
and hungry. They kick vigorously
toward the smell of soup. Fed,

smiling again, they run to play
in a yard where the earth is polished
from so many feet. The guests follow,
well-lunched and laughing as they watch
a relay race of letters delivered
to a little green mailbox; braided rings
tossed around a stick; and run-sheep-run,
only in this country, it's a rabbit

with cardboard ears, running for his
life to the sizzle of a young teacher's
tambourine, then found and hugged–
not eaten–and settled down for a nap
to singsong music as the visitors
feel dreamy, charmed, seeing themselves
playing those games years ago
in vacant lots, backyards. Home.

TIGER HILL

No tiger. Just a hill with teahouse
next to wedding-cake pagoda
that leans too much for climbing.
Our faces shine above our fragrant
teacups as we turn to view
through latticed windows ancient
gardens blue with haze below.

We find instead bouquets of Chinese
faces pressed at dusty windowpanes,
peering into our cage, at us, the latest
tigers. We study the tea leaves, mutter
to ourselves how communism is turning
common folk away. We ask our guide,
Why don't you let those people in?

Mr. Wu adjusts his smile of uncommon
charm and quotes the numbers, says
so many feet would trample lovely
teahouse flat. We swallow hard, gaze
at carvings above our heads, ask
him something simpler. Why pagodas
perched on hills? His airy answer:

to offer flying spirits a roosting place.
Our tea begins to taste like weeds. We rise
and gather souvenirs, avoid the stare
of leather faces as we walk a thousand
steps down Tiger Hill, where spirits
hover, pilgrims keep on climbing,
and we return to trampled earth.

VISION AT TAI-SHAN MOUNTAIN

I'm doubtful, restless, on this journey
upward with Buddhist pilgrims to Tai-Shan seeking
whatever mountain covered with cloud can give.

Here at the midway station, the summit's foot,
westerners gasp at miles of stairway carved
into rock, a tower of Babel, a Jacob's ladder,
spotted with toiling figures. For tourists

there's another way: a sky tram with rickety
gondola packed and swaying across chasms toward
the sacred peak beyond mist. I stay behind, feet
wanting earth. Instead I pace the road past booths
of hawkers, then follow a path away from the crowd,

looking for hummingbirds, five-leafed ginseng.
Litter grows on the slopes, pecked by squawking
magpies. The path leads to a hut on a cliff
where two men carry a load of cabbages on a pole
through a narrow door. They argue, go sideways,
heads tumble and roll. I want to laugh but there's

too much that's human in it, earthbound like me,
no place to turn. The long-tailed magpies soar
into the abyss as I edge to trail's end, only to find
a privy, foul as a harpy's nest. *Back!* the birds
cry. I turn, clouds break, the mountain flashes
a mirror signal from a temple where saffron monks hum
beyond all I know. Then mist moves over like a hand.

FOUR

Looking for Grace

WHERE IT HURTS

In memory's interior eye this old girl
is new, a school child with white flower face
ready for Easter, shiny shoes tapdancing
on cracks down a sidewalk, skirt twirling
like a parasol, singing, *Mirror, mirror*
on the wall, let my father say I'm pretty,

not you look like my sister Grace, that curse
to make a daughter old as a Chinese aunt, flat
photograph always staring, gray as a church
with closed doors hiding something sinful.
But she's ugly! the girl cries with a false
truth no little lady should tell. Her chest

tightens as she gets into the family car,
hugs herself in the backseat, ribs hurting
from big sister's scornful elbow. Silent
father sits at the wheel, never looks back.
This old girl wants to jump out, but it's too late.
Then love's brass looking-glass goes dark.

The Gift Mirror

My Chinese Aunt
Grace with her letters full
of floods and famine and children
stiffening under sycamores
while missionaries
carved
their Sunday lamb

threw her Bible away
and sent our family
a gift: this
mirror of amethyst and jade.

Looking for
her picture lost inside
these attic boxes
I find instead
myself
staring out of the gift mirror–

a missionary
surrounded
by grapes and leaves,
asking

Who *is*
this old girl?

The Hook

An old man made of terra cotta
always fishes with good luck
from the edge of my father's desk.
The little carp he catches
smiles as if the line that dangles him
could suddenly plunge deep enough
to go home, to find the artist

who made him, the merchant
who sold him, the young man
who bought him and tossed
this treasure across the sea
to hook my father and me.

Unsent Postcard to My Father

This is Tianjin, cold and harsh, Aunt Grace's
old city. I want you to know K and I witnessed
the memorial to stand up for her American family.
For you. We didn't know what all the words meant,
but Papa, you can be proud of your sister. She
was a good wife and mother. In the eulogy
they said she was a great teacher and patriot.
So what, if she chose real China instead of your
American dream and married a man who called
himself "heathen." She's saved, I hope, no matter
what she believed. Isn't that what true grace
means? As you always used to say, Papa,
Rest assured.   Please.

Something Lost

Once I saw on TV an old
Chinese woman with her voice
shaking tell how she fled the communists
during the civil war, when rich people like her
left everything behind, taking only the clothes
on their backs–plus the valuables
they hid underneath–to seek
freedom. She saw

herself a heroine, daring
to abandon most of her worldly belongings
for the cause of an abstraction. An admirable risk,
perhaps, except later I learned, when she dropped
like a small paper sack slipping from
a great bundle, the news that among
the things she left behind was
a baby–her only

daughter. I think
her child comes home in my suitcase,
maybe in everyone's suitcase. She keeps on coming,
growing smaller, hard and bright as a pearl.
None of us knows what to do with her.
She's everything we ever did wrong,
failed to do, loved–
but not enough.

The Key

A locked suitcase.
Tiny gold key. Lost.

Want to turn the lock,
open everything up,

burrow inside stuffing,
throw out silks, beads, letters,

dig down under thick wool,
find something hard,

shiny, the ache
of a gold tooth at night,

key itself
locked inside the suitcase.

Chisel, knife, axe.
Sister. Father.

Unpacking the Suitcase

Everything in order
when I packed my bag:
thick-soled shoes, cotton undershirts,
wool scarf for walking in bitter off-season cold,
two pairs of eyeglasses to guard against loss,
binoculars to help me see
even farther, the guidebook,
pills. I numbered

the days, baedekered and timetabled
my heart, wound it up tight with spirals
of cities, rivers and mountains, pagodas and shrines–
cocooning myself from the one day of mourning I feared
would drown me with voices and faces, this funeral
journey disguised as
a trip. Now I come

home, open the suitcase, put away
silks, souvenirs, unsent postcards, coins
now worthless, small notebooks spotted with rain. Things
I didn't see inside the suitcase start rising up
dark as a mountain of rags: clothes I knew
well as my own skin turning to ruins
I dig through, mole-like, hands
into claws, raking what's
buried all the way
down to where
it hurts.

FOUND SNAPSHOT: THE YEAR HIS SISTER LEFT

A young father pulls
back his small daughter
in a wooden swing,
a plank and two ropes
hung from an oak.

It's early evening
after work. He looks
tired, with his tie loose,
his white shirt open
at the neck. He holds

her steady and close
to him, pausing this
instant before he
lets her swoop out
among leaves and sky

back to his arms again.
The little girl's face
is complete as a rose.
For this one moment
her father belongs

only to her. He will
always stand there
to hold her back,
let her swing out,
bring her home.

REMEMBERING THE THREE GORGES

for my father

The Yangtze River
flows wide and narrow,
narrow and wide,
like an ache that comes
and goes, a pain

in the shoulder
from holding your hand
for hours as you squeezed
along a narrow passage
I couldn't see, like
a pilot guiding a ship

blind. It was my third
night watching. My right
arm bent over the steel
bars to cling to what
was left of you, giving
me this ache that

stays with me
a year later, mark
of a grief I thought
had already loosened
its hold, the way
a flood withdraws,
leaving the shore

damaged, the way
your spirit flew
away from me, home
to your mountains,
far from the river's
changing path.

THE ROPE

Last night my father came back.
At first I saw him from a distance
across a long valley with no trees
beside the Great Wall. My mother
and sister held onto me, watching
him walk slowly down a steep path
behind a man who led him with a rope
as if my father were a colt. The man,
a stranger, wore a tight, dark suit.
Father's white shirt hung loose
with no tie except the rope. He
looked young again, innocent
of all that has happened.

Tonight they return, come closer.
The man vanishes and Father starts
to climb with us into a blue sedan,
our old family car. Mother flutters,
Is it really you? Oh, I'm so glad
to see you again. Then her face
shadows. If he's alive, he will
have to die again. I watch myself
reach forward, try to take hold
of the rope, tell him there's
no room. I can't speak.

MISSING IN CHINA

Sudden moonlight steals my father from me.
These nightly visions of his death must end.
Another woman lies down in my place

awake. She wears a copy of my face.
Her skin is torn, a scar she could not mend.
Her open eyelids steal my father from me

with foreign dreams suggesting prophecy,
a lonely death some distant God might send.
A jealous woman lies awake in place

of daughter's innocence. Buried memory
weaves a rope from silken dresses, blends
flags and flowers, steals my father from me

as I dream a death I would not hope to see
except that life itself decrees an end.
Again his sister rises in my place,

the one who left her brother without grace.
Her missing face is mine. My dreams pretend
a foreign country stole my father from me.
A jealous child is waking in my place.

FOR THOSE WHO DREAM OF CRANES

After a painting by Song Feng Guang

1 *Jinan, China*

They wait for you at night
in a thicket of bamboo. Snow
falls around them. Their feathers
rustle in light wind like secrets.
They are talking about you. Beaks
click like yellow knitting needles.
Circle-eyes pull you with invisible
strings onto their ground to turn you
into part of the ceremony. Watch how
they bow, lift up long stick-legs,
set down feet as if casting small nets.
Now they are calling, dancing. Their
feathered crests nod, white wings
billow in moonlight. Then daybreak.
You awake alone, heavy. Silence.
A thicket. Ghosts of cranes.

2 *Stonington, Michigan*

In late August near home, as the sun
drops its red coin into a slot of
black trees, sandhill cranes float
down into the new-mown hayfield
where they pace and strut, nearly
tall as deer, dark gray, ghostly,
making no sound as they feed, ready
to leave for winter. Last spring
you heard them coming, a muttering
beyond the lake like something small.
Closer, they grew monstrous, voices
loud as dry wood dropped in a box.
They passed over, bound for their hidden
nesting place. Tonight you watch them
again before they vanish tomorrow,
coming, going, sure as the sun.

3 *Jinan*

Steel cranes lean over this city,
piling up giant buildings where
low brick houses with courtyards
used to sprawl and tumble, where
backyard fields of corn and cabbage
reached toward the countryside. Now
these great featherless birds haunt
the new skyline, as if everything
depended on height, concrete, money.
Images of sacred cranes still grace
the city pavement, the ancient form.
The artist at the university quickly
brushes them in traditional form to help
feed his family. But in this scroll,
his favorite, painted slowly at night,
cranes live as they should, forever.

4 *Jinan. Stonington.*

In the thicket again, white cranes
wait. You enter, empty-handed.
From inside the puzzle of branches
you see vast plains where farmers
cut corn stalks by hand. Hunched
families drag rakes over dry soil
to plant wheat for millions of mouths.
You turn. Beyond bamboo, the hayfield
near home. Gray cranes feed in first
light. They gather to fly over miles where
bird-like machines worth armies of farmers
eat corn. Wings pump high into cloud,
over cities already jagged with steel.
Inside the maze, you learn the language,
begin the ceremony. Gray brothers,
fly safely. White spirits, speak.

GRATEFUL ACKNOWLEDGMENT IS MADE TO THE FOLLOWING PUBLIcations in which these poems, some of them in different forms, have appeared:

Helicon Nine: "Two Women Leaving Beijing," "City of Dust and Water" under the title "In a Far City." *The Helicon Reader:* "Two Women Leaving Beijing." *Iris:* "The Gift Mirror," "Hawthorns," "Two Women Leaving Beijing." *Images*: "For the Chinese People, Who See the Same Stars" under the title "Sight." *Nankai University Journal*: "For the Chinese People, Who See the Same Stars" ("Sight," in Chinese translation). *Contemporary Michigan Poetry* (anthology): "Two Women Leaving Beijing," "City of Dust and Water" under the title "In a Far City." *Poets On*: "Nearly" under the title "Glimpses." *Parting Gifts*: "Chinavision." *Christian Science Monitor*: "The Hook" under the title of "Simple Surprises." *Eclectic Literary Forum*: "Paper Flowers." *Writers at Work*: "Mr. Yuan's Two Joys." *Borderlands: Texas Poetry Review*: "Partings." *Hawaii Pacific Review*: "The Guest Chair at the University" and "Bamboo" under the title "The Senior Center at Jinan." *Americas Review:* "Two Women Leaving Beijing," First Prize Winner, 1995, and "Mr. Yuan's Two Joys." *Connecticut Review*: "The Rope." *Doors of the Morning* (anthology): "Paper Flowers" (Co-winner of the Sandburg-Livesay Award, Canada, 1997). *Waiting for You to Speak* (anthology, Sandburg-Livesay Award, 1999): "Chinese Puzzle" and "In a Far City." *The MacGuffin:* "Ghost City."

Some of the above poems and additional poems appeared in the following chapbooks: *A Bridge to China* (Plattsburgh, NY: Hardwood Books, 1983); *The Green Heart* (Normal, IL: Illinois State University, 1994), which won the Illinois Writers, Inc., competition for 1993; and *Chinavision* (Greensboro, NC: March Street Press, 1995).

Many of these poems were written with the assistance of grants from the American Association of University Women and the Michigan Council for the Arts. They grew out of travel in China for purposes of family reconciliation, research, and tourism in 1980, 1993, and 1995. A documentary account of the life of Grace Divine Liu, the author's aunt who lives in these poems, may be found in *Grace in China: An American Women Beyond the Great Wall, 1934–1974* (Montgomery, AL: Black Belt Press, 1999) by Eleanor Cooper and William Liu, in which "A Bridge to China" is included as an epigraph.

The author wishes to thank Roger Weingarten of the M.F.A. program at Vermont College for his perennial acumen and generosity during the development of this collection. Others who helped early in the work's progress were Heather McHugh, Mark Doty, Mekeel McBride, Leslie Ullman, and Pattiann Rogers. The late William Matthews gave important encouragement near the end of the project. Thanks also to friends and colleagues Carol Hackenbruch, Larry Leffel, Anne Ohman Youngs, Mary Joy Johnson, and Deanna Pickard, and to my son-in-law and colleague, Kurt Ayau. Special gratitude to the McCallie, Divine, Liu, and Benedict families in whose stories and images these poems are grounded.

ABOUT THE AUTHOR

Elinor Benedict, a native of Tennessee and graduate of Duke University, earned an M.A. in English from Wright State University, Ohio and an M.F.A. in Writing from Vermont College. She has won several journalism prizes, the *Mademoiselle* Fiction Prize, a Michigan Council for the Arts Award, and an Editor's Grant from the Coordinating Council of Literary Magazines (now CLMP). As a writing teacher and founding editor of *Passages North* from 1979-1989, she has encouraged many emerging writers.

Her poems have appeared in magazines and in five chapbooks, including three with a Chinese theme. This body of work began to develop in 1980 when she traveled to China with her daughter to attend her aunt's memorial "rehabilitation" after the Cultural Revolution. In 1993 and 1995 she returned to China for seminars and tours.

Her most recent chapbook, *The Tree Between Us* (March Street Press), deals with life in the Upper Peninsula of Michigan, where she lives with her husband among trees, lakes, and snow. They also spend time in Naples, Florida and travel whenever possible, often visiting their three adult children and seven grandchildren.

ABOUT THE MAY SWENSON POETRY AWARD

The May Swenson Poetry Award was named for May Swenson, and honors her as one of America's most provocative, insouciant, and vital poets. During her long career, May was loved and praised by writers from virtually every major school of poetry. In John Hollander's words, she was "one of our few unquestionably major poets." She left a legacy of nearly fifty years of writing when she died in 1989.

May Swenson lived most of her adult life in New York City, the center of poetry writing and publishing in her day. But she is buried in Logan, Utah, her birthplace and hometown.